Impressions of *Seine-et-Marne*

Text
Jean-François Caltot

Photography
Jean-Pierre Chasseau and photographers from the Seine-et-Marne and Île-de-France

ÉDITIONS DANIEL BRIAND

Table of contents

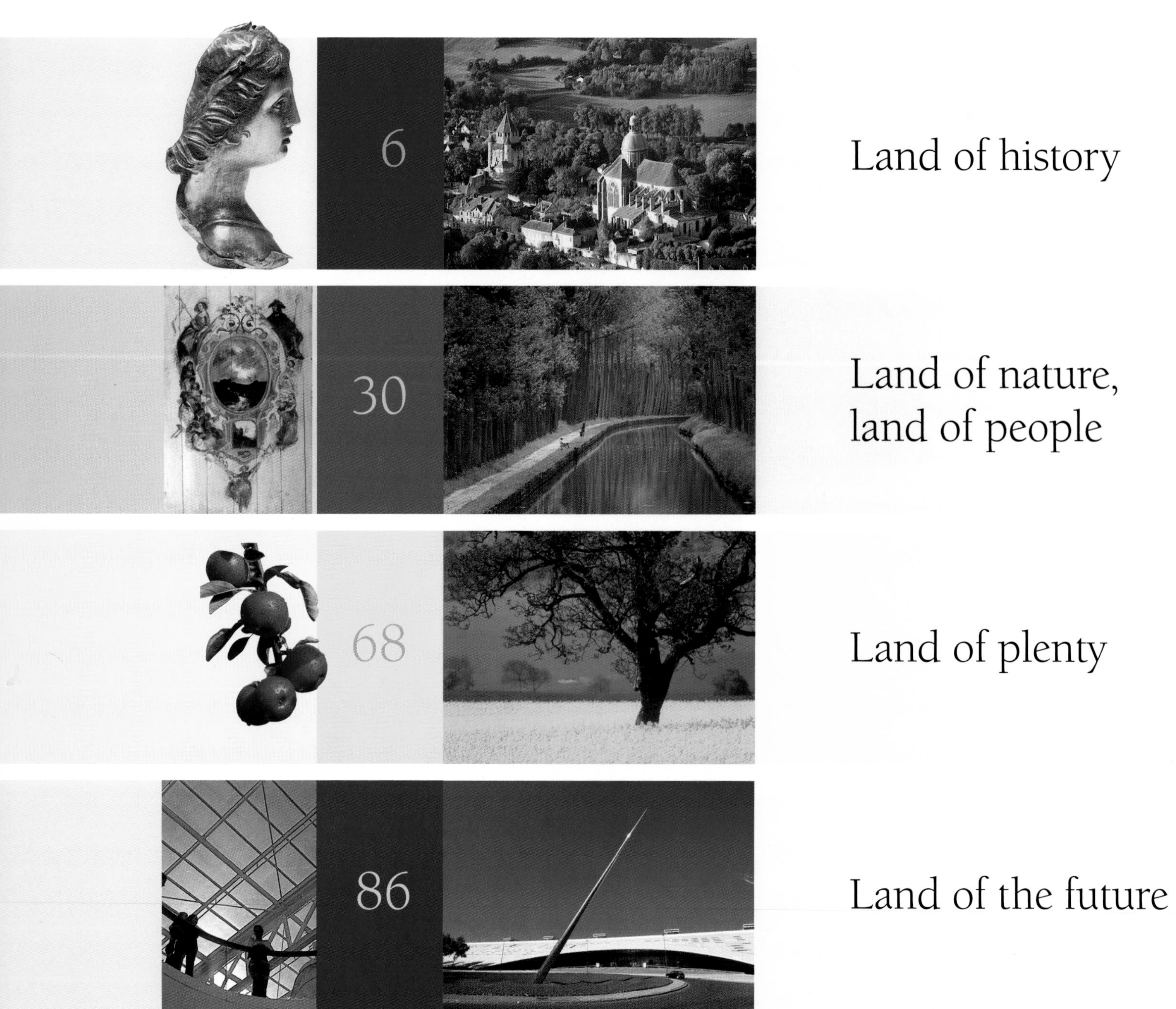

Impressions of Seine-et-Marne

"Farewell" Courtyard at Fontainebleau Castle.

As a new territory unfolds, one cannot but wonder: "what are the makings of this land?" Which features truly shape a region, a place, a department? Its geographical relief? Its outer limits? The people who live there? In the case of the Seine-et-Marne, the answer lies in the sum of the centuries making up its history and the different forms of its geography.

When they set up camp on the banks of the Seine, on the edge of Bassée, the Magdalenian reindeer hunters probably did not realize they were the first settlers in this future Seine-et-Marne. They were simply there tracking game. Similarly, many centuries on, when civilisation appeared in this corner of Gaul, it is on the banks of the two rivers, the Marne and the Seine, that it took root, along these natural, practical paths of communication.

natural paths of communication

Yet can one say that it is the two rivers, whence the name, that shaped the Seine-et-Marne? One would be overlooking the two territories that stretch north and south of the two waterways together with the vast central plain that links them together like a fertile "Mesopotamia". Three regions with different soils which offer this department a wealth of natural resources.

So, two rivers and the plains they irrigate? We are getting close to the answer, but are still forgetting an essential factor: the people who settled the Seine-et-Marne. Those who discovered the extraordinarily fertile soil and decided to clear the forests to sow wheat, the only real source of wealth up until the middle of the 19th century. Would Paris have become the capital if it had not been able to draw on the prosperity and bountifulness of this bread basket crossed by two peaceful rivers plied by overflowing barges? Not even the Beauce can make such a claim.

the wealth of the soil

The wealth of the soil naturally spawned many other riches, starting with solid boroughs built of beautiful stone and powerful towns, some of which became royal, or, in one case, imperial cities. This interaction, first called barter, trade, then commerce and finally business, turned this vast territory, which now constitutes half the Île-de-France region, into a hub. And indeed, that is the second *raison d'être* of this department. Certain patterns of behaviour never seem to grow old; is there much difference between the tradesmen at the Champagne fairs, whose stalls heeped with cloth and furs made the fortune of Provins in the 12th century, and the logistics experts of today who choose this buffer zone between Paris and Europe for their giant warehouses? Just a matter of scale - plus, unfortunately, the look of the buildings...

two rivers fertile plains and open valleys

Two rivers then, fertile plains, open valleys for stock-raising, here and there underground deposits of building stone, silica, clay (and even oil, discovered far more recently) and, finally, people who decided at the time of the Revolution to create this administrative department out of the royal *bailliages*, taking over all or part of former natural regions like Brie, Gâtine, Champagne, France, Multien. A unique case in Île-de-France, this layout has not been changed since that time. The Seine-et-Marne has remained a great green scarf, stamped with two symmetrical "7"s, surrounding the capital and its region on the east as though to protect them from the ill winds of history.

A protective rampart therefore as in September 1914 when the banks of the Ourcq gave support to the desperate counter-offensive launched by General Joffre against the German armies about to enter Paris; but also, an outstretched hand, wide open in a gesture of welcome. Certain kings of France set up house there, endowing Melun or Château-Landon with the envied status of royal towns. The Flemish or

Lombard merchants built the wealth of Provins. The Italian Renaissance artists imported by Francis I created the universal splendor of Fontainebleau. The first reformed church of France was located in Meaux, home also to the first Protestant martyr before becoming a bastion of the Counter Reformation. A man by the name of Nicolas Fouquet burnt his wings there trying to rival with the most powerful monarch in Vaux-le-Vicomte. Errant painters, reacting to the official academism, projected a simple village of woodcutters to the forefront of the world stage. An enviable pedigree and tradition that attracted any number of artists, scholars, men of letters, ranging from Primatice to Sisley, including Pasteur, Voltaire, Lamartine, Mallarmé, Mac Orlan or Vercors. The latter, who founded the "Editions de Minuit" and became a "Seine-et-Marnais" at heart late in life, summed up the rich departmental heritage in a text called "Ma Brie". He wrote, in particular, "*Such wealth in a single department is a hymn to the glory of a whole province*".

artists,
scholars, men of letters

This vast wealth inherited from the past complies nicely with the requirements of modern life in order better to fulfil the aspirations of over one million two hundred thousand inhabitants resolutely turned to the future, mindful of the fact they live in an exceptional area in the capital's region. For the phenomenon continues with the means and at the pace of our times: people no longer talk of royal towns but of "new towns"; as for the dream turrets of the Disneyland Paris castle, their economic weight is as great as the powerful ramparts of Provins at the time of Count Thibaud...

an exceptional area

6 Land of his

A RICH PAST LIES BURIED IN THE SEINE-ET-MARNE; sifting its soil yields endless relics, tragic souvenirs of wars and invasions or valuable legacies from periods of peace and prosperity. In the Marne or Bassée quarries, excavations unearth centuries-old silex tools while farmers on the banks of the Ourcq carefully build mounds of ploughed up "75" cartridges or German *shrapnells* on the edge of their fields. Archeologists, together with the quarriers and developers, have joined forces to deal with all the discoveries linked to the many worksites. Preventive archeology has thus developed in a particularly active manner in a booming department like the Seine-et-Marne.

Ternary motif bronze torque.
Second Iron Age, 4th-3rd century B.C.
Found in Marolles-sur-Seine.
ÎLE-DE-FRANCE PREHISTORY MUSEUM IN NEMOURS.

Bronze jewelry discovered in Grisy-sur-Seine.
End of the Bronze Age.
Around 1 000 B.C.
ÎLE-DE-FRANCE PREHISTORY MUSEUM IN NEMOURS.

Upper left:
Carved biface,
Old Stone Age, around 300/200 000 B.C.
ÎLE-DE-FRANCE PREHISTORY MUSEUM IN NEMOURS.

Neolithic ceramics from Noyen-sur-Seine.
Around 4 000 B.C.
ÎLE-DE-FRANCE PREHISTORY MUSEUM IN NEMOURS.

tory

Because of its geographic position on the eastern flank of the capital in addition to its relief, the Seine-et-Marne has given French history any number of famous battlefields. From the Roman general, Labienus, marching on Lutetia, to Emperor Napoleon, in February 1814, to General Joffre defending Paris against the German advance a century later, the list of these many bloodbaths that stained our furrows is long. Yet, once peace returns, the towns and cities prosper, rich homes, fortified farms, castles and abbeys are built, the arts flourish, thought matures. Land of kings, land of lords, land of people...

Bronze Age warrior's helmet. Around 1 000 B.C. Île-de-France Prehistory Museum in Nemours.

Bust of Apollo, silver and gold (height: 7,6 cm), 1st or 2nd century A.D.
La Bauve Site in Meaux.

La Bauve Gallo-Roman sanctuary

Huge complex used as a place of worship, built at the end of the 1st or beginning of the 2nd century; lasted until the end of 4th century A.D. Located half-way up a hill north-east of Meaux. Comprises a double enclosure with 130 metre sides, still standing to a height in excess of 3 metres, which mark the limits of a vast esplanade.

The western part of the site contains a huge temple with a double, symetrical centre. Excavations have yielded a large number of Gallic and Roman coins, ornaments and animal bones linked to sacrificial rites.

The Middle Ages

Medieval times are the golden age for the Seine-et-Marne. This is the period that produced its most beautiful items of religious art and its most famous castles, town centres and certain traditions. The stamp is ever present, from Lagny to Melun, royal town, from Nemours where Capetian France stopped to Brie-Comte-Robert, where Jeanne d'Évreux' castle rose, from Fontainebleau, hunting venue for Louis VII, to Provins. Thanks to these riches, the department now has two sites listed as World Heritage by UNESCO.

Provins ramparts.

Provins medieval fête.

Provins

THE PRESTIGIOUS INVENTORY of World Heritage carefully drawn up by UNESCO received a precious addition in 2001. The third millenium dawned auspiciously on this medieval town, a unique testimony to the trading cities of the 12th century. The town boasts a fabulous heritage of civil, religious and military architecture. No fewer than fifty-eight historical monuments and, above all, perfect consistency in its activities at the peak of its splendour under the reign of the Champagne counts. Be it the city walls, Cesar's Tower, underground galleries or superb churches, Provins today is a particularly dynamic venue for tourists. An international stop-over for all those who appreciate ancient, lively sites.

Inside Saint-Quiriace Collegiate church and Cesar's Tower.

" Provins Eagles " show.

Blandy-les-Tours

A SHOWCASE OF THE MIDDLE AGES! People come from throughout Ile-de-France to admire this citadel, unique in the region. It conjures up life at the time of the Hundred Years' War far better than a history book. In fact, this old 13th century fortified castle nearly ended up in ruins before the General Council purchased it in 1992. It went on to do a spectacular piece of restoration, turning the citadel into a unique example of medieval military architecture at the very heart of a charming village in Ancœur country.

Jouarre

What remains of the abbey founded by Adon in 630 is St. Paul's crypt, built by St. Agilbert. This vestige of a funerary basilica that vanished in the 15th century is one of the best preserved Merovingian buildings in Europe. A room with three naves contains the sarcophagi of the abbey founders, including that of Adon, St. Telchide, the first abbess, and St. Agilbert.

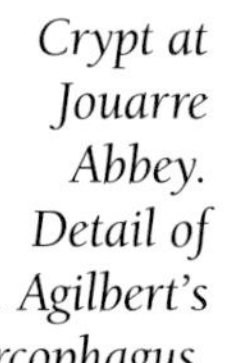

Crypt at Jouarre Abbey. Detail of St. Agilbert's sarcophagus.

Recumbant figure: St. Osanne (13th century).

Head of a king.
Vicomté Museum.

Nestled in the centre of town, the florid Gothic Saint-Aspais Church (1515) is one of its kind. In addition to its beautiful outer facades with flying buttresses, it contains some superb stained glass windows.

Melun

The "Briard Lutetia", thus called because of the resemblance between its island location and that of its big neighbour further down the river, was founded in Gallo-Roman times. Julius Cesar refers to it as Metlosedum when telling the tale of General Labienus in his Gallic War. In the Middle Ages, it became a royal city under Robert the Pious (970-1031), son of the founder of the Capetian dynasty. It remained so for three centuries. Life revolved around the island, Saint-Étienne, flanked by a religious complex to the east (Notre-Dame church) and the royal castle to the west, which is no longer standing.

Detail of Saint-Aspais church façade.

View of medieval Melun.
Vicomté Museum.

Coulommiers

THIS LARGE VILLAGE DEVELOPED in the Middle Ages under the aegis of the counts of Champagne, to whom it belonged like its prestigious neighbour, Provins. It inherited a Templar commandery from the Crusades following a bequest of land to the Order in 1128. When the Order of the Knights Templar was dissolved, the commandery passed into the hands of the Knights of Malta. Over the centuries, commander's lodgings, a chapel and dovecot were added to the complex, a unique domain in the region.

Commandery of the Knights Templar, which became a commandery of the Knights of Malta, and medieval garden.

Brie-Comte-Robert

SEVEN LEAGUES FROM PARIS, Brie-Comte-Robert, as the name indicates, was the seigneury of Count Robert de Dreux as of 1136. Its castle, built in the 12th century, overlooked the plain thanks to a 33 metre tower and its Hôtel-Dieu (13th century) welcomed travellers and the indigent. The town displays its medieval past in the magnificent Gothic façade of the Hôtel-Dieu, the castle precincts, Saint-Etienne church and many other scattered vestiges.

Sculpted arch of the Hôtel-Dieu and view of the precincts of the old castle.

Lagny-sur-Marne

This other Champagne fair city failed to preserve the immense heritage of its rival, Provins, but nonetheless bears witness to these prosperous times in Brie, from the 12th to the 13th centuries. Notre-Dame des Ardents is a vast abbey church complete with ambulatory and side chapels on a scale worthy of a cathedral, unfortunately unfinished for lack of means. 44 of the 100 windows nonetheless contain illustrations, in mainly 19th century stained glass. Joan of Arc passed through the town twice, in 1429 and 1430, on her way to the Loire and is said to have wrought a miracle by reviving a newborn who had died before being christened.

Light filtered by the stained glass turns Notre-Dame des Ardents iridescent pink.

Half-timbered house.

Castle and keep reflected in the Loing.

Nemours

A proud 12th century castle turned into a museum, St. John the Baptist Church, also from the 12th century, with some beautiful stained glass windows, "little moats" along the ramparts that used to protect the town, and the vestiges of Joye gate still bear witness to the medieval past of Nemours. After the fire that destroyed it during the Hundred Years' War, the town acquired new momentum thanks to the duchy created in 1404. An important stopping place on RN 7, Nemours has retained the charm of ancient city with its old streets.

Meaux

Cesar named the capital of the Meldes (Gallic people) *Iatinum*. In Gallo-Roman times, it was located on one of the four main Roman roads (Sens-Boulogne). Meaux still contains impressive vestiges of this period like the antique theatre, ramparts and nearby site of La Bauve...

The city centre boasts the beautiful Saint-Étienne Cathedral (1170-1540) and the 12th century episcopal city; major work in the 17th century turned the latter into an aristocratic abode endowed with splendid gardens.

It was also at this time (1681) that Jacques-Bénigne Bossuet (1627-1704) became bishop of the diocese. The Meaux Eagle – prelate, renowned preacher, writer – was also tutor to the young Dauphin, Louis (future Sun King) aged 9, before supporting the religious policy implemented by his former pupil against the Protestants (Revocation of the Edict of Nantes).

General view of Meaux cathedral and details.

Land of lords and courtiers

SO MANY CASTLES makes one think of Touraine. Prestigious homes were built here from medieval times up to the bourgeois 19th century by counts, dukes, marquesses, but also a good dozen kings and two emperors, the princes of banking and business, daring entrepreneurs, great state civil servants. Their keeps and turrets are the lasting signs of their glorious past.

Fontainebleau Castle National Domain.

Fontainebleau

TALKING OF FONTAINEBLEAU PALACE, inherited from a long line of crowned heads, Napoleon uttered this phrase that has remained famous: "*Here is the true dwelling of kings, the house of centuries*".

Paraphrasing the Emperor inspired by other circumstances, one might say today, about Fontainebleau: "*From the height of this palace, nine centuries look upon us* ".

Throne of Napoleon I.

Carp pond.

Francis I Gallery.

Diane Gallery.

From the Capetians to Napoleonic times, the majestic building superimposes eras, influences and styles to produce one of the most comprehensive testimonies to French history. From Louis VII in the 12th century to Napoleon III, it is here that the country's fate was often decided. Philip the Fair died there and Louis XIII was born here, Francis I "invented" the Renaissance at Fontainebleau and Napoleon bid farewell from the palace. Palace and gardens have been declared world heritage. *(Museum and National Domain).*

Napoleon Museum: on display since 1986 are superb collections concerning the emperor and his family (paintings, furniture, apparel, arms).

Chinese Museum: the right wing of the palace contains a number of surprising collector's items, Oriental art and furniture collected by Empress Eugénie in her Chinese museum during the Second Empire.

Stucco-work in the Duchess of Étampes' room.

Vaux-le-Vicomte

ONE OF THE STATUES IN THE PARK represents a squirrel in the claws of a lion - a visionary fable considering what befell the famous owner, Nicolas Fouquet, whose emblem was a squirrel.

Young Louis XIV had good reason to be jealous of his financial superintendant's castle, seen for the first time the evening of the grand, fatal party on 17 August 1661, which immediately caused Fouquet to fall into disfavour.

Ceiling in
the Salon des muses.

Today, however, over and above the elegance of the building, what is truly breathtaking is the layout of the gardens. They are the epitome of science at the time (water, physical and optical engineering) and the perfect embodiment of French esthetics in the era of Louis XIV. Three geniuses created the site: Le Vau for the architecture, Le Nôtre for the gardens, Le Brun for the decoration. An absolute masterpiece which, no doubt, inspired Versailles and the idea that a palace can be used as an instrument of power.

(Private castle open for visits).

Ferrières

Like the incredible Anglo-Norman "folly" at Gretz-Armainvilliers (now in private hands) or even Champs-sur-Marne, Ferrières bears witness to the era of the princes of finance in the 19th century. A mixture of different styles (Anglo-Italian-French) cleverly combined by the architect, Paxton, Ferrières is like a dream rising from the lake that reflects its image, in the middle of a huge English-style park. A tasteful construction commissioned by James de Rothschild, which welcomed a number of famous visitors like Prince Otto Von Bismarck. Before being rebuilt by Paxton, the castle was home to Joseph Fouché, minister of the Empire. *(Private castle open for visits).*

Staircase of honour and details in numerous styles.

Champs-sur-Marne

BY A QUIRK OF HISTORY, this classical castle built by a financier (Poisson de Bourvallais) right at the beginning of the 18th century finally ended up, at the end of the 19th century, in the hands of another family of financiers and industrialists, the Cahen d'Anver, who bequeathed it to the State. In the meantime, the majestic building was home to the Marquess of Pompadour. In the '60s, "Champs" welcomed many dignitaries, particularly African, invited by Général de Gaulle as part of the decolonisation policy. Visitors may admire its beautifully furnished rooms and its gardens, designed by a student of Le Nôtre and renovated by Duchêne. *(National monument).*

Detail of the Chinese drawing-room.

Blue boudoir.

Guermantes

It is, of course, Proust's books that made this beautiful country house world famous. The author of "In search of lost time" did not, however, visit the places that housed any number of parliamentarians and financiers like Law, the inventor of paper money. The initial layout was designed by Robert de Cotte; the architect Paulin Pondre added the famous gallery, called "the useless beauty", in purely Versailles-like vein, much later, at the end of the 17th century. *(Private castle open for visits).*

Sigy

The moats surrounding this magnificent rural home cover nearly one hectar and create the impression the castle was built on an island. The layout of the building, constructed in a forested region in the south-eastern part of the department, near Donnemarie-Dontilly, has remained virtually unchanged since the 15th century, flanked by four watch-towers, at each angle. *(Private castle).*

Bourron-Marlotte

This aristocratic abode from the early 17th century was home to a king: Stanislas Leczinski, the deposed king of Poland. It drew inspiration from its prestigious neighbour, Fontainebleau, copying the horseshoe shape of its staircase, designed by Jean Androuet du Cerceau. *(Private castle).*

Nangis

The beautiful building that now houses the town hall (since 1860) is, in fact, a wing of the medieval castle built in the 12th century to protect merchants travelling from Paris to Provins and dismantled at the end of the 18th century. In 1814, Napoleon, in the middle of the French campaign, spent the night in Nangis. La Motte-Beauvoir castle is flanked by outbuildings protected by moats, which were then turned into farms and now house the cultural facilities of the commune. This ensemble is rounded off by Saint-Martin et Saint-Magne church, built in the 13th century just next door.

Fleury-en-Bière

HENRY IV AND HIS MINISTER SULLY, the "Grande Mademoiselle", Richelieu and the Duchess of Berry stayed in this magnificent complex built as of 1550 for Cosme Clausse, Henry II's secretary of royal finances. Fleury castle's sandstone and quarry stone facades decorated with brick lend this home a majestic appearance. The gardens are outstanding. *(Private castle).*

Le Vivier

THE LORDS OF GARLANDE, squires of Tournan, have been the registered owners of Vivier Castle, of which only the romantic ruins remain, since the 12th century. Sold subsequently to Charles de Valois, brother of Philip the Fair, the residence remained part of the royal estate until the Revolution. Its chapel, like the Sainte-Chapelle in Paris, contained a relic of the holy cross.

(Private estate).

Jossigny

THE ELEGANT PROPORTIONS of this French-style castle are due to Jacques Hardouin-Mansard, the last of a great dynasty of architects, who built it for Claude-François des Graviers, whose coat of arms adorns the magnificent gate of honour. *(National monument undergoing restoration).*

THROUGH THE AGES

-10 000
Pincevent reindeer hunters and large number of prehistoric settlements, not far from the rivers.

-52
Labienus, Cesar's general, looks for a ford in Melun to cross the Seine and continue up to Lutetia.

584
Assassination of Chilpéric, king of Soissons and grandson of Clovis, in Chelles.

632
Founding of the Merovingian abbey, Notre-Dame de Jouarre, by Adon.

1358
End of the Jacquerie in Meaux. Execution of the mayor and destruction of the fortress.

1419
Assassination of John the Fearless in Montereau.

1540
First French Protestant community in Meaux.

1685
Revocation of the Edict of Nantes signed in Fontainebleau on the 18th October.

1790
On the 4th March, the Constituent Assembly defined the shape of the Seine-et-Marne department by decree.

1793
Uprising in the east of the department, called "the little Briard Vendée", in the name of freedom of worship.

1814
Last stand by Emperor Napoleon against the coalition army at the battle of Montereau.

1914
The time of the great battles.

1944
General Patton's offensive and liberation of the department in August.

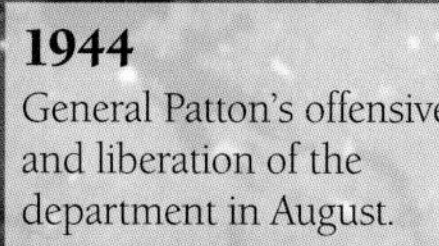

The time of the great battles

"*Wheatfields and battlefields*". That is how French history refers to the Brie. In September 1914, on the banks of the Ourcq, the village of Lescherolles constitutes the most forward position reached by the German army in its advance. One month after general mobilisation, Von Kluck and Von Bulow's armies were no more than thirty kilometres from Paris. On September 6, general Joffre signed his legendary order of the day: "*No one shall retreat. A regiment that cannot move forward shall, come what may, maintain its position and be killed on the spot*". The 6th French army in blue jackets and red trousers began its counter-offensive on the banks of the Ourcq. Losses were tremendous in the freshly cut wheatfields; Lieutenant Charles Péguy died in Villeroy, the first of the four hundred writers killed in the Great War. On the 11th September, this first round in the Battle of the Marne pushed the front back by sixty kilometres. Paris had been saved.

Land of nature,

WHILE NATURE IS NOTHING WITHOUT PEOPLE, the opposite is also true. Of all the Île-de-France departments, the Seine-et-Marne is no doubt the one that has best understood and respected this natural complementarity. The department's 58 300 square kilometers, three quarters of which resemble a well-tended

land of people

garden, bear witness to this fact, home to as many differences as the trained eye of the visitor seeks to discover. While the Seine-et-Marne seen from a plane approaching the landing strip at Roissy-Charles-de-Gaulle Airport appears flat and uniform, an in-depth visit of its component parts prove this to be untrue. Plains, granted, but not "a plain", as the area is punctuated by valleys and forests making up a great, Harlequin-like mosaic. The two rivers that join in a V like two fingers on a hand, together with their tributaries, shape this discrete but very real relief. This geographical relief ranges from the occasionally steep banks of the Marne in the north to the central plateau, which then opens into the vast, undulating plain in the south stretching towards the Beauce. Between the two rivers is the Brie plateau. 514 communes are located on this colourful checkerboard and most have remained villages. The urban ramparts running along the west like a very dense segment of a circle gradually give way to little strings of hamlets nestled against their churches, creating this *urban* blend that makes the area the "*green lung*" of Île-de-France.

The great forests

ONE FIFTH OF THE SURFACE AREA is covered by forests, that is, approximately 125 000 hectars. In this vast "green lung", the forest of Fontainebleau stands out with 25 000 hectars containing a vast array of species, huge expanses of sand and rockery, history and mystery. However, the royal wood, which also includes Trois Pignons, should not lead one to forget the other private or state forests: Ferrières, Gretz-Armainvilliers, Villefermoy, Jouy, Léchelle, La Commanderie, Nanteau-sur-Lunain, Sénart or Sourdun. A huge ecological and economic heritage worth preserving.

Forest crossroads with obelisk and sign post.

Pond in Ferrières forest.

The forest of Fontainebleau

THE FOREST HAS BEEN LEGENDARY since the mid 19th century when painters fondly turned it into a mysterious, fantastic setting for their naturalist pictures. Long before, the kings had chosen it as a hunting ground, and today, eleven million visitors each year come to walk or do any number of sports. This ancient sea in the Tertiary Period left a surprising geological heritage of sand arenas and sandstone outcrops. The wood, where 5 685 varieties of plants grow and 6 600 species of animals live, enjoys, with its biological reservoirs, a special status called "protection forest".

"It is not just a forest that I should like to see, it is Fontainebleau..."
MARCEL PROUST

Autumn mists above Larchant.

Stag troating.

Fairy pond.

Along the waters

1 800 KILOMETERS of more or less domesticated rivers. The Seine-et-Marne owes a great deal to its waterways, starting with its name and a great deal of its cultural and economic development in the course of history.
Although these rivers, these waterways, these canals have now in part been deprived of their activity with the decline of inland water transport, they are still major assets for the towns through which they flow and key components of both heritage and landscape.

Saint-Mammès is the Seine-et-Marne river port "par excellence", *where a certain image of inland water transport remains with its freight exchange and sailor bars. The junction of the Seine and Loing was the city's wealth. Indeed, it still lives according to the pace of calls to port and sailors coming up from Bourgogne and those coming down from Holland, who tell their tales in a Simenon style atmosphere.*

1821909L
LYJA
LYJA

Moret-sur-Loing

MORET-SUR-LOING became a royal town thanks to the early Capetian reigns. It has retained all its harmony as a medieval city since those times. Walking along the banks of the Loing, one can readily understand why Sisley felt particularly inspired by this city.

Grez-sur-Loing

THE STEEP GRADIENT OF THE LOING as it passes through Grez-sur-Loing generates a strong enough current for a mill. This medieval village also attracted painters from around the world as of the 19th century and was viewed as a sanctuary by a school of Japanese artists like Seiki Kuroda or Chu Asai.

Thomery is the village adopted by Rosa Bonheur, a painter of animals, whose studio is now a museum.

Samois

ONCE A YEAR, the village comemorates Django Reinhardt's riffs and gears up for a famous gypsy jazz outdoor festival. The gypsy guitar player now rests in the little cemetery in the village where he lived for several years.

Vulaines

THE POET, STÉPHANE MALLARMÉ, chose this "*verdant haven where a river sings*" to settle next to the Seine in Valvins. His house is now a departmental museum which pays tribute to the author of the cast of the dice which "*will never do away with chance*".

Thomery

WHEN THE MEANS of preserving the bunches of grapes that accounted for the fortune of this big village was discovered in the 19th century, the town became a real river port that transported the Chasselas grapes to Paris. Invented by Baptiste Larpenteur, the "*green stalk*" technique kept the stem of the bunches fresh in a container full of water.

THE SEINE AND THE YONNE

Upstream of Montereau, the Seine becomes the "Little Seine". At this stage in its path, the river that irrigates Paris has not yet received the valuable flow of the Yonne and still remains a small river. In this respect, the observations of a very serious geographer, published a few decades ago, establish that at the junction in Montereau, the rate of flow in the Yonne is greater than the Seine. Logically, it is therefore the Seine that flows into the Yonne and not the other way round. Yet can one say that the Yonne runs through Paris and flows into the Channel at Le Havre? That would upset many a geographic and historical reference.

The "affolantes" were born in the 19th century of the desire of wealthy Parisians to escape to the waterside or forest edge thanks to a recent invention: the railroad.

The pace of life in Montereau was long dictated by its pottery works, which produced the legendary crockery used by our grand-mothers, "Flora" and its inimitable blue hue.

Montereau.

Black-necked grebe and swans taking wing.

La Bassée

As the names indicates, this is a low-lying region where the Seine tends to get lost a bit and turns into pools, marshes and backwaters. The flood plain rich in calcarious gravel made many a quarrier rich and turned the Seine-et-Marne into the leading producer of aggregate in Île-de-France. It is also a paradise for many species of migrant birds and sedentary waders in addition to fishermen, who have made some of the best catches here in the fishing history of the department.

Extraction of calcarious gravel.

THE MARNE

UNLIKE ITS TWIN SISTER, the Seine, which flows rapidly towards Paris, the Marne takes its time. It meanders along leisurely, in a series of loops sculpted in a more pronounced landscape. The Marne is thus a tranquil counterpoint to what the Seine offers in terms of inland water transport activity. It is a well-known paradise for fishermen and the ideal place for Sundays by the riverbank and "*a little glass of white wine under the bowers*".

What would the Marne be without its "guinguettes" (cafés with music and dancing)? Here, in Précy-sur-Marne, the village where Yves Duteil is mayor and where the singer Barbara once lived.

Trilbardou

The impressive mechanisms for raising the water level in the canal above are historic buildings from the 19th century, symbols of the mechanical achievements of the era.

*Like Saint-Martin canal,
the Chalifert canal also runs
underground when the geographical relief
so requires.*

Noisiel

MEUNIER CHOCOLATE-FACTORY in Noisiel backs on to the Marne, which it used as a source of energy. This historic factory is currently the Nestlé head office and its phalanstery has been converted into public premises and a forum for various activities.

*Overshadowed by the impressive silhouette
of Houssoy Castle,
the pristine village of Crouy-sur-Ourcq
owes its fortune, in the 19th century,
to the store ships
that transported merchandise
on the canal.*

Ourcq canal

THE CITY OF PARIS commissioned the building of the Ourcq canal, which started in the 17th century. It ends at La Villette. The canal had a two-fold function: not only to provide for the transporting of merchandise from the east (particularly wood for heating and construction), but above all to supply the capital with the water it sorely lacked. Ourcq canal is now most sought-after for country walks along the towpath and small barge cruises between the various villages on its banks.

Wash-houses and mills

MANY VILLAGES IN SEINE-ET-MARNE have a wash-house. While all these “gossip areas” no longer resonate with the conversations of washerwomen and their paddles, the communes are trying to restore these vestiges of the past.

Tilly wash-house.

Souppes-sur-Loing wash-house.

Another typically local phenomenon, the paddle mill, so necessary in a grain-growing area. There were many dotted along the rivers as in Melun, where two flour mills were active in the 19th century, and in Meaux, with Cornillon mill downstream of the old bridge located near the cathedral. Some were even to be found along little rivers like the Hyères, whose course was punctuated by milling facilities.

Fleury-en-Bière wash-house.

Nemours mill.

Charming villages and landscapes

THE SYMBOL OF THE SEINE-ET-MARNE could be a stone bell-tower surrounded by a few houses nestling in the fold of an immense plain of wheat: the famous vision of "calm strength". Of the 514 communes making up the Seine-et-Marne, most are villages that have succesfully preserved the very endearing charm of hamlets where nothing has changed. Some are on the edge of forests, the most famous being Barbizon, others by rivers like Samois, while others again are located on the plain that produced their wealth.

A frontier village between the Loiret and Seine-et-Marne, Beaumont-du-Gâtinais was founded by the Beaumont family around the year one thousand. The superb 18th century half-timbered hall located on the village square was used to sell wheat, as the two granaries on either side attest.

Hall in Beaumont-du-Gâtinais.

La Genevraye
With its original church perched on a hill, the village looks over the Loing and its canal just above. Two locks lent some activity to the commune in the past prior to the building of a dynamite factory.

Barbizon

A WOODCUTTERS' VILLAGE known throughout the world. Only painters could thus spread the word. The Barbizon School was born in the mid 19th century following the break with classical tradition.
Théodore Rousseau, Diaz de la Peña or Jean-François Millet went directly to the source of their inspiration, painting light at sunset,

Sideboard painted at Ganne Inn.

JEAN-FRANÇOIS MILLET. *The Gleaners.*

JULES-LOUIS-PHILIPPE COIGNET. *Painters "on the motif".*

GEORGES GASSIES. *Théodore Rousseau's House.*

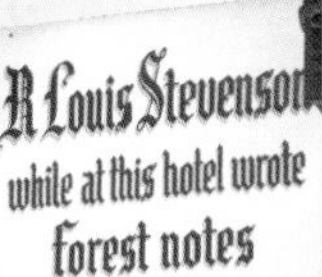

Ganne Inn.

peasants at work, flocks returning home or the mystery of the forest. They were assisted in their endeavour by the chemical progress made with their "colours" that could henceforth be transported. Their impecunious outings forever immortalised Father Ganne's inn as they painted its walls and furniture; the inn is now a museum. International fame did the rest, turning the hamlet into a residential and tourist village.

Detail of a panel painted by Diaz de la Peña and Théodore Rousseau in the artists' dining room. The two characters at the top come from the opera "La Bohème"; the libretto was written here...

Égreville

Each year, just before Christmas, Égreville hall (16th century) is home to a traditional fattened poultry fair. It is a leap back in time in the ancient stone hall covered with a huge mossy roof, where the gabbling of the turkeys vies with the breeders' conversations. The high point of the day is the plumage contest sponsored by the "*Trousseurs de gâtinaises*" Brotherhood. Égreville was also the village adopted by the musician, Jules Massenet, and the sculptor, Antoine Bourdelle; his son-in-law's home contains some beautiful reproductions of his work.

Égreville hall.

Sculptures by Antoine Bourdelle.

Larchant

THE BEAUTIFUL, PARTLY RUINED TOWER of St. Mathurin and the surrounding village seem to emerge from the green depths of the forest. A vision straight from the past like the 13th century door of the "Last Judgement" decorates the church. The village was known both near and afar in the Middle Ages because of its position at the junction of two major antique routes. People went through Larchant to go to Rome or Santiago de Compostela as well as to get into favour with St. Mathurin, who delivered the mad and possessed (pilgrimage attested to since the 9th century). Several kings, the last being Henry IV, also visited Larchant. A short distance from the village are superb rocky outcrops like Dame Jouanne, the highest in Île-de-France.

Château-Landon

IT IS ON ONE OF THE RARE SPURS in the area that the Gâtinais counts decided to locate their capital. Overlooking the sinuous Fusain, the town nestles against several towers and spires and the remains of Saint-Séverin abbey. Château-Landon has remained the agricultural capital made rich by wheat. In fact, each period in history marked the destiny of the commune. Pre-history, first, followed by the Gallo-Roman period with the construction of an *oppidum*, the Merovingian period with, according to legend, the death of St. Séverin, the Middle Ages when Château-Landon became a royal town, and finally, modern times with intense grain-based activities and sandstone mining, particularly to build the Arc de Triomphe.

Pouilly-le-Fort

Difficult nowadays to reach Pouilly-le-Fort, a hamlet in Vert-Saint-Denis, because of the network of motorways surrounding it. A 14th century castle still bears witness to the importance of the site during the Middle Ages. Louis Pasteur lived here and conducted his experiments on anthrax. A "state education" museum depicts our grandfathers' school.

Burcy

The village located on a hill looks over the huge plain that stretches gently towards the Beauce. Its pretty 12th century church boasts several stained glass windows designed by Jean-Michel Folon in 1997, a tribute by the artist to his adopted village

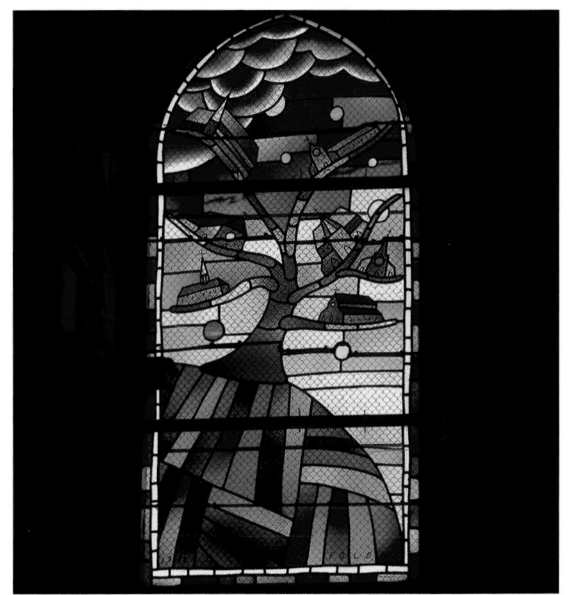

Saint-Méry

THE HILLSIDE on which it is built adds to the charm of this village with outstandingly harmonious architecture that even modern times have not managed to alter.

Samoreau

ONE OF THE JEWELS OF THE COMMUNE is its 12th century tithe barn that came under the authority of Saint-Germain-des-Prés abbey in Paris. The roof frame dates from the 15th century.

Champeaux

Champeaux is of course famous for Saint-Martin, its collegiate church, a veritable 12th and 13th century gem. In the choir, the sculpted wood stalls, which feature "misericords" that made it possible to rest while remaining standing during prayers, still seem to be waiting for the canons.

Inside and bell-tower of Saint-Martin collegiate church.

The "misericords".

Lourps

Lourps chapel stands out no doubt because of its location on the top of a hillock overlooking the Voulzie. It collapsed in part in 1966 and benefitted from twelve years of restoration work. Its walls boast a number of superb frescoes.

Donnemarie-Dontilly

The Provinois church circuit offers a comprehensive view of sacred art in the region.

Time seems to leave no trace in the town centre. The medieval garden of Donnemarie is located in the former parish cementery. It was landscaped by Christophe Grunenwald and represents the ideal view of paradise, with twelve rectangles for the twelve apostles and, at the intersection between its central alleys, the Cross of Christ, conveying the ancient idea of the four rivers of paradise.

Saint-Loup-de-Naud

ALL THAT CURRENTLY REMAINS is the abbey church of the Benedictine priory founded in 981. Like an image from the past, the church stands in the middle of its village built on a hillside. Its door, unique in Île-de-France, is typical of early Gothic period with column-like statues and outstanding sculptures.

Rampillon

IN THE 12TH CENTURY, Rampillon marked the border between Champenoise Brie and French Brie and indeed resembles a fortified place with its very rare fortified church. The western door of the church is like a medieval "cartoon" with scenes depicting various forms of work in the fields, surmounted, of course, by views of the apostles.

Monastic life

One of the oldest abbeys in France was founded in Jouarre in the early 600s in the steps of St. Colomban, who came from Ireland. One thousand four hundred years later, Benedictine nuns still occupy the premises, attesting to the persistance and deep roots of the religious communities in the area. In the course of history, Brie and Gâtinais welcomed a host of monasteries, whose wealth was commensurate with the bountifulness of the surrounding land.

Franciscains convent in Provins.

Interior of Cercanceaux abbey and detail of a capital.

Insignia of the Brotherhood of Monastic Products.

Statue of Christ at Jouarre abbey.

A first wave of foundations dates back to the beginning of Christianization in Jouarre and in Château-Landon (Saint-Séverin), Faremoutiers, Chelles, Lagny, Rebais. The renewal of the communities came later, in the 12th and 13th centuries, with the Cistercian revolution which led to the founding of the great abbeys in Pont-aux-Dames, Jouy, Cercanceaux, Barbeau, Preuilly, in addition to Lys abbey. A new order was taking shape; it was to last up until the Revolution.

Old Lys Royal Abbey in Dammarie-les-Lys.

Doue

THE HILLOCK on which this little village in Rebais canton, in a perfect state of preserve, is perched is the highest point in Seine-et-Marne. This is no doubt the reason why people were interested in the site as of prehistoric times, before building a fortified place in the Middle Ages, fought over during the Hundred Years' War. St. Martin ostensibly went through Doue and is portrayed in a beautiful polychrome stone statue in the church that bears his name. The Doue fiefdom was long owned by the Juvénal des Oursins family; one of the last lords was officer in turn of the royal cavalry followed by the revolutionary army before becoming general of the Empire and, in that capacity, Empress Joséphine's equerry.

Saint-Martin church and polychrome statue of the saint.

Museum of the Lands of Seine-et-Marne.

Saint-Cyr-sur-Morin

THE VILLAGE was long a "rustic" extension of Montmartre, thanks to its most famous guest, the writer and lyrics composer Pierre Mac Orlan, author of "*Quai des Brumes*", who introduced artistic and literary celebrities like Roland Dorgelès, Francis Carco, Max Jacob or Maurice Vlaminck to Saint-Cyr-sur-Morin. The village, nestled in a deep valley of *Petit* Morin, offers an atypical insight into a "Vosges-like" Seine-et-Marne with its geographic relief, forests, Micheline rail-car and Museum of popular arts and traditions, which boasts an impressive collection of tools and was founded by the General Council in 1995 in the former *La Moderne* inn.

Crécy-la-Chapelle

NICKNAMED the "Briard Venice", indicative of the charm exuded by this large village built on the banks of the Morin, which was a merchant and agricultural town before turning into a country venue in the 19th century, with painters like Camille Corot, in particular, in residence.

Saint-Fiacre

Pilgrims attracted by the reputation of St. Fiacre were so numerous that the Irish monk was authorised to enlarge his domain by the area he could dig in a single day. The village was born of pilgrimage. According to legend, the holy man's spade worked so quickly that day that people talked of a miracle, and even witchcraft, which Fiacre was able to defend himself against. He gained from this agricultural feat the title of patron saint of gardeners. An annual pilgrimage is dedicated to this saintly healer, to whom "green thumbs" throughout Europe remain devoted.

National and international fête of the patron saint in Saint-Fiacre en Brie in September.

St. Fiacre in Avon, the statue of the patron saint borne with pride.

Morin villages

The villages nestled between *Grand* and *Petit* Morin belong to what is familarly called the "Little Briard Switzerland": a land of forests, undulating countryside and babbling brooks. Willow used to be grown, turning the valley peasants into basket weavers who produced highly sought-after baskets and boxes. The hydro-power of the rivers was also used to make paper. Morin country is now greatly appreciated by hikers because of its many walks...

View of Jouy-sur-Morin from the road.

Villeneuve-sur-Bellot church.

Willow fields in Morin country.

Church porches and typical bell-towers

Brie churches are certainly in the image of the locality where they stand: deeply rooted, if one can put it thus, and solidly anchored to the plain. Very often Romanesque, their massive stone arches face the harsh winds which occasionally sweep the plain, without too many spires or pretentious bell-towers. Most of these modest country churches nonetheless boast a range of arts prevailing at the time. Porches with semicircular openings or decorated with statues like at Saint-Loup-de-Naud, lintels and doors sculpted with scenes from the Gospel or profane country life, fortifications like in Rampillon, stained glass windows in different styles produced by the master glass-makers at different periods in history, and even the very contemporary creations of Jean-Michel Folon in Burcy.

Door of the Église de la Nativité (13th century) in Villeneuve-le-Comte.

Western door of Rampillon church.

When the contemporary espouses the old...

Provins possibly owes its initial success as a place of pilgrimage to St. Ayoul, whose relics were discovered in a most timely way in 996. The church dedicated to the saint is in any event a pure delight due to the superimposition of styles between the 12th and 16th centuries. The 20th is not left out thanks to the sculptor Georges Jeanclos who, in 1990, following the collapse of the Glory of Christ decorating the tympanum, incorporated his contemporary work among the column-like statues from the 12th century.

Saint-Loup-de-Naud church (12th century): door characteristic of early Gothic sculpture, influenced by the one in Chartres cathedral.

Porch of Saint-Ayoul church in Provins.

Arbonne-la-forêt church.

Bell-tower of Ury church.

Bell-tower of Burcy church.

Tourism in a natural setting

IT IS OFFICIALLY PROCLAIMED that Seine-et-Marne is the playing field the inhabitants of Île-de-France prefer. The figures for local tourism are there to prove the point, placing the department near the top of the list, just after Paris, as the region of France that attracts the largest number of tourists. This achievement is obviously due to the two Disney parks, but not exclusively...

The Seine-et-Marne is a huge territory where Parisians like to come and stretch their legs but also enrich their minds. From rock-climbing to castle visits, from wind-surfing to the discovery of museums, from golf to spiritual meditation in the abbeys or churches, Seine-et-Marne is an extremely diversified place to stay that is, moreover, well endowed with hotels, restaurants and lodgings of all kinds. A change of scenery "two coaching inns" from Paris.

Horse-trecking

ELEVEN THOUSAND Seine-et-Marne inhabitants hold equestrian sport licences, but it is estimated that 25 000 people come to ride each year in the department, mainly to go on outings or trecks. One hundred and fifty-seven clubs or stud farms are there to serve them.

River tourism

TOURISM IS BOOMING not only on the rivers but also the hundreds of kilometres of canals and waterways, thanks to the little barges for which no licence is required and the numerous stopping places organised by the communes.

Leisure centres

THERE ARE EIGHT SUCH CENTRES, ranging from Jablines to Torcy, including Vaires-sur-Marne, Saint-Rémy-de-la-Vanne, la Grande-Paroisse, Bois-le-Roi, Buthiers and Souppes-sur-Loing, where one can not only indulge in virtually every sport but also rest.

Land of plen

LIKE ALL AREAS STEEPED in tradition, the Seine-et-Marne has many natural or man-made resources handed down over the centuries, that constitute its rich heritage. One can wonder about the relationship between the wheat, the numerous cheeses, the poultry, but also the glass and pottery industries, or even the villages made of beautifully chiseled stone. All these features have something in common: they are home grown or produced. In fact, throughout its history and up until the second half of the 20th century, the Seine-et-Marne remained a “son of the land”, content with its bountiful local resources and a few processing industries. Relatively well endowed in these areas, in addition to its traditional activities, it never really needed the kind of industrialisation foisted like a graft on a tree deemed not to yield enough fruit.

The turning point came in the ‘50s, however, when the department was signaled out for some leading high-tech enterprises; its location, on the threshold of the capital, attracted major schools (*grandes écoles*), international communications, new cities and an international tourist complex. There is no mistaking the fact that when the designers of Disneyland Paris chose Marne-la-Vallée in 1985, they were thinking of the future of this vast, pristine area just outside

Paris, the prime tourist destination in the world and veritable springboard to nascent Europe. People have now realised that the booster engine of eastern Paris is located in the Seine-et-Marne and keeps the whole Île-de-France region at cruising speed.

A land of wheat

Of the 340 thousand hectars of agricultural land in the department, 75% is used to grow grain. Seine-et-Marne thus ranks second, after the Eure-et-Loir, in this activity. The average size of cereal farms is 140 hectars, with annual yields of roughly 80 to 90 quintals a hectar. This specialisation does not prevent the Seine-et-Marne from also producing barley (36 000 hectars), beetroot (30 000 hectars), rapeseed and maize (26 000 hectars).

A land of stock-raising

Further to the requirements of the CAP (Common Agricultural Policy), farmers have (re)discovered the meaning of the word diversification. They are thus following the paths of their ancestors, reviving high standard animal husbandry like *Grand cru* lamb (which replaces 19th century Paris lamb), Île-de-France beef, milk production indispensible for AOC cheeses, poultry which, in the recent past, was still present on all the farms. 6 100 horses are bred in Seine-et-Marne, of which 2 400 on farms. 750 brood mares have also been counted, that is one third of the total figure for Île-de-France, who give birth to 70% thoroughbreds.

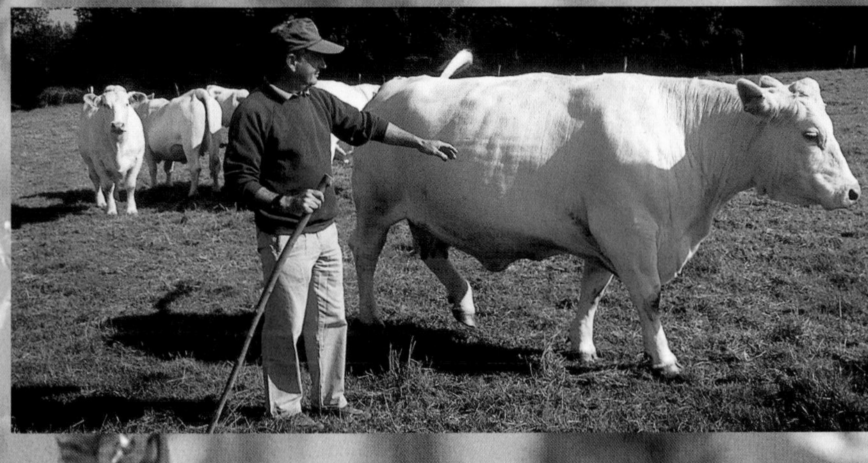

Fields and orchards

ABOUT two hundred market gardeners still work with greenhouses or in the open field in Seine-et-Marne, particularly in the Pays de Bière whose vegetable produce is highly appreciated in Paris markets.

Picking

Born of the spirit of agricultural diversification, picking attracts a growing number of consumers who want to know where the content of their plate comes from. An amusing way to do one's shopping!

Specialties

Cheeses

ACCORDING TO THE SAYING "Cheese of the kings and king of the cheeses", Brie has always stood out in the course of history, and often because of the kings. From Robert the Pious, the excommunicated king who imposed it on his table at Melun court just before the year one thousand to Louis XVI who took a light meal of Brie before fleeing to Varenne, without forgetting Henry IV who discovered it in Coulommiers together with Margot, his queen, Brie is omnipresent.

In fact, one should really talk about Brie in the plural because eight different varieties have been identified, only two of which have an AOC: Meaux and Melun.

Brie de Meaux is of course better known and more widely produced than its cousin from Melun, which is smaller in diametre and also stronger tasting.

Old Brie moulds made of willow.
SAINT-CYR MUSEUM.

The famous Fontainebleau, a cheese dessert, in its immaculate muslin.

Moulding, draining and drying of Brie cheeses.

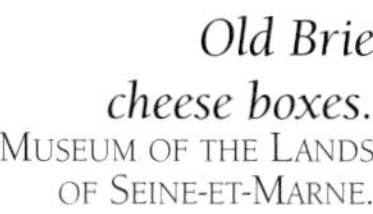

Old Brie cheese boxes.
Museum of the Lands of Seine-et-Marne.

Brie de Meaux.

Brie de Melun Brotherhood.

Brie de Meaux Brotherhood.

Brie de Montereau is somewhere between the first two in terms of taste. Brie de Nangis is made in small mould that gives it its characteristic shape. Coulommiers is a variety with a pale yellow interior when mature.

Farm Brie must at all costs be made where milking takes place, which makes it rarer but also more authentic. Potted Brie is in fact a goat cheese that is left to dry for twenty-five days.

Fougerus is a soft cheese with a florid brown rind, sold with a fernleaf. In addition to the traditional Bries, there are the "triple creams", namely Gratte-paille, Butte de Doue, Vignelais (in its vine-leaf), Fontainebleau and Explorateur from Coulommiers, thus named in honour of the discoverer of the headwaters of the Amazon, Bertrand Flornoy.

Coulommiers.

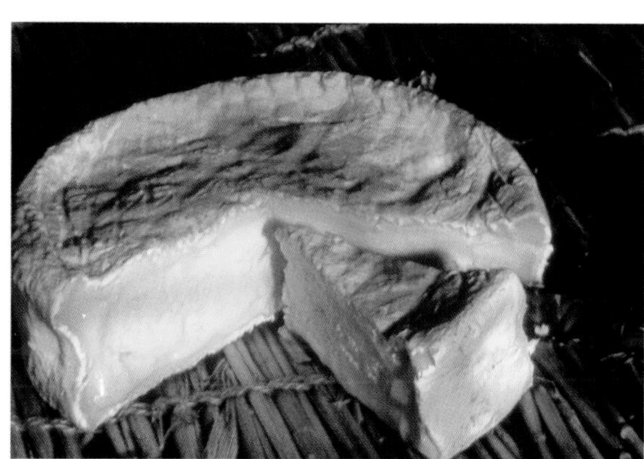

Barley sugar

One of the oldest confectionaries in France was created in Moret thanks to Benedictine nuns who, as of the 17th century, produced a sugarcane and barley candy to treat sore throats. The tradition has been upheld and expanded to include an elixir, a brotherhood and a barley sugar museum that tells the tale of this delicacy.

Nemours poppies

Poppy flower candy was born in Nemours around 1850 in Mr. Desserey's shop, rue de Paris.

Honey

THE LEGENDARY HONEY FROM THE GÂTINAIS comes from the fodder crops grown in the 19th century, mixed with a host of flowers. Bees in the area used these flowers and particularly the "*saint-fouin*" to make honey with such a distinctive scent that it is only found in the Gâtinais and is still made today.

Member of the Barley Sugar Brotherhood.

Rose de Provins

IT IS SAID that Thibaut IV of Champagne returned from the Crusades around 1240 and brought a rose bush back from Jerusalem. A tradition was to arise from this tale, that of rose petal jam which is now the gourmet symbol of the good old town of Provins.

Mustard

WHEN ONE SPEAKS OF MUSTARD, one obviously thinks of Dijon, but also Meaux, with a gastronomic secret, thanks to the religious orders in the 17th century, that has never been revealed. Meaux mustard, of which 1,5 million pots are produced each year, is widely exported and greatly appreciated throughout the world.

Beers

TO MAKE BEER, one needs barley, which is in no short supply in Seine-et-Marne. Hardly surprising therefore that three brewers produced highly appreciated varieties of Brie and Gâtinais beer.

Ciders

A LAND OF ORCHARDS, the Seine-et-Marne could hardly but produce cider with a few varieties reputed for their flowery aromas.

Champagne

A FEW WINE PRODUCERS grow champagne grapes along a narrow strip of land bordering on the Marne and hold an AOC label.

Seine-et-Marne flavoured menu

concocted by
Jean-Jacques Malleret
chef in Seine-et-Marne

Crécy soup
(called after Crécy-la-Chappelle)

For 4:
1 onion, 6 medium-sized carrots, 3 leeks,
5 potatoes, one spoonful of thick cream,
one bunch of chervil and 2 slices of white bread.

Finely chop the onion, the white part of the leeks and the carrots. Melt the butter in a heavy saucepan and braise the vegetables. Dice the potatoes. When the leeks and onion are slightly brown, add the potatoes. Pour in enough water to cover the vegetables by 2 cm. Add salt and pepper and cook without a lid. Blend the vegetables as soon as they are cooked. Add 50 g of butter and one spoonful of thick cream. Correct the seasoning. Before serving your soup, fry squares of white bread in oil and scatter the croutons on the surface of the soup, adding the tops of the chervil.

Briard-style pullet

For 4:
one 2,5 kg pullet (to be ordered from a farm in Seine-et-Marne), cleaned, boned and cut into pieces, 2 onions, 2 carrots, 1 bottle of Briard cider, 100 g of Meaux mustard, 80 g of flour, 200 g of thick cream, 20 cl oil, salt and pepper.

Dice the onions and carrots and fry them in a casserole with oil. When the vegetables start to go brown, add the pieces of pullet and fry them also. When the poultry is nicely browned, add salt, pepper and sprinkle with flour. Mix well. Do not let the flour brown. Add enough cider fully to cover the pieces of meat. Cover and simmer gently. When cooked, remove the pieces of meat and keep them hot. Strain the sauce. In another bowl, add the Meaux mustard and some of the sauce, mix and add the thick cream to obtain an unctuous sauce. Check the seasoning and pour the sauce over the pieces of pullet. This dish can be served with *endives au gratin* or boiled potatoes.

Brie in flaky pastry on a bed of mesclun

For 4:
4 portions of Brie de Meaux or de Melun (a bit stronger), flaky pastry dough, one egg, 4 teaspoons of thick cream.

Roll the pastry into a big square 2,5 to 3 mm thick. Cut it into eight 15 cm squares. Place the portions of Brie in the centre of 4 of the squares and shape into small pyramids. Drop a teaspoonful of thick cream onto each pyramid. Separate the white of the egg from the yolk; beat the yolk with a drop of water. Using a brush, apply the yolk to the edges of the pastry. Place the remaining 4 squares of pastry on top of the filled squares and fold over the edges. Brush the remaining egg yolk onto the pastry. Place in a hot oven for 12 to 15 minutes. Serve on a bed of mesclun seasoned with hazel nut oil vinaigrette sauce.

Fontainebleau with red fruit sauce

For 4:
4 Fontainebleau, 1 kg red fruit (in season),
1 kg sugar, 1 litre water.

To make the sauce, prepare a transparent syrup by mixing 1 litre of water and 1 kg sugar and bringing to the boil. Cook the red fruit, blend and strain the mixture, pressing down on the fruit. Mix the juice with the syrup and let cool in the refrigerator. Carefully place the Fontainebleau in the middle of a plate, pour the sauce over it and sprinkle with fresh fruit.

Fortified farms

LONG BEFORE BEING CALLED "GREEN GOLD", wheat was a coveted asset. In troubled times, the farms that grew and stored wheat naturally protected themselves. As of the 13th century, the first fortified farms appeared in Brie, like stone ships moored on the plain, where harvest and harvesters could be protected. These fortresses surrounded by walls were organised like autarkic lines of defense with sheep-folds, stables and often dovecots; over the centuries, they turned into magnificent manor houses standing proudly in the middle of their estate. Époisses or Mainpincien near Mormant, Nolongues near Jouarre, Marets, Esmans, Bois-Hébert and Guignes are outstanding examples, anchored forever in the middle of the wheatfields and guardians of the grain-growing tradition in the department.

Amirault farm.

Interior of the dovecot on Époisses estate.

Époisses estate.

Esmans farm.

Nolongues farm.

Mills and dovecots

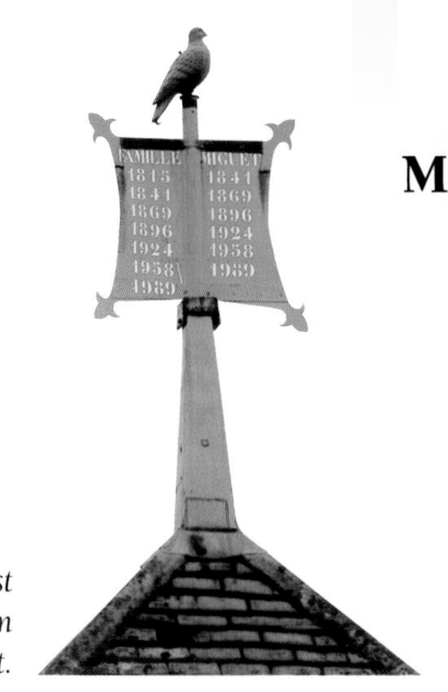

Roof-crest of Miguet farm dovecot.

Windmill in Gastin.

Dovecot at Jouy abbey.

Dovecot at La Recette farm.

Underground riches

OVER THIRTEEN MILLION TONNES of material of all sorts are extracted from the ground in Seine-et-Marne each year, ranging from aggregate for construction and roads to clay for pottery works, including sand for glass-making, highly appreciated by glass-blowers in Venice, and millstone used to build so many typical homes. The Seine-et-Marne also produced sandstone for historical monuments, gypsum for plaster work and the last few drops of oil in the region east of Paris.

Earthenware

The first pottery works in Montereau were created in 1719. Run by the English, it boomed in the 19th century and became mechanised. It then merged with the Creil factories and closed down in 1955.
A particularly well-endowed museum pays tribute to the works today and a potter now upholds the tradition. A very pretty style of crockery was also produced in Rubelles, near Melun, from 1839 to 1859.

Clay

IN THE '70S, around seven hundred clay miners or "grey faces" still mined the highly reputed Provins clay used to manufacture industrial pottery or as an electrical insulator. Long-gone ancestors extracted this material used for wool fulling back in the Middle Ages.

Bezanleu tile works began its activities in 1836.

Sand

THIRTY-FIVE MILLION YEARS AGO, the sea withdrew and deposited sandbanks which, in the course of time, thanks to the action of freshwater, limestone and forces of compression deep within the earth, have reached us in the form of particularly pure, silica-rich expanses of sand. This sand is processed and used to manufacture glass for television screens, optics and artistic use.

Sandstone

AROUND 1830, a thousand quarriers worked in Fontainebleau forest on deposits like that of Haut-Mont. They extracted this sedimentary rock made of grains of quartz and sand that is a popular material in the construction industry. A great part of the paving stones in Paris come from Fontainebleau in addition to the stone for many historic monuments like the Arc de Triomphe, for example.

The sandstone details of the Grotte des Pins at Fontainebleau Castle seem to echo the animal sculptures shaped by nature like the "Dog Head Rock" at Trois Pignons (Triple Spur) here in Fontainebleau forest.

Land of the

LAND OF THE PAST, the Seine-et-Marne is notwithstanding a land of the future. In keeping with a destiny begun two thousand years ago on the banks of its two rivers, it still has the same assets, viewed, however, from a different angle - that of modern times.

Roads which today are called autoroutes - three in all - in addition to regional speedways, high-speed trains, including an interconnected network. Space, which is sorely lacking in the capital, is liberally available in the Seine-et-Marne, both to set up activities and taste the joys of intact nature. And finally, manpower, with a moderate population growth (1 250 000 inhabitants), which implies one of the best job-inhabitant ratios in Île-de-France.

At the heart of Cité Descartes, the ESIEE premises in the shape of a computer keyboard.

future

"Grandes Écoles"

As a result of its population growth, the Seine-et-Marne is well equipped with teaching structures. This is particularly true of the university world, where it has benefitted from the structuring effect of decentralisation. Marne-la-Vallée has, over the years, become a bastion of "grandes écoles" at the Cité Descartes technopolis, with prestigious facilities like the ESIEE (Higher School for Electronic and Electromagnetic Engineering) and the École Nationale des Ponts et Chaussées in addition to a fully fledged university. In the south, Sénart, Melun and Fontainebleau have widened their offering with university institutes, an offshoot of the law and economic sciences faculty of Panthéon-Assas, or again the very famous business school, INSEAD, whose American-style campus is located on the edge of Fontainebleau forest.

École Nationale des Ponts et Chaussées. Cité Descartes.

INSEAD (Institut Européen d'Administration des Affaires) in Fontainebleau.

Lavoisier University, Marne-la-Vallée.

Disneyland® Resort Paris

Disneyland® Hotel .

EURO DISNEY S.C.A. has developed three major poles in Val d'Europe, which constitute a unique success. The following have thus been built: the prime European tourist destination based on two theme parks (112 million visitors since 1992), a new town with superior quality of life, inspired by the Île-de-France region, and a business pole right in the heart of the city with an international, innovative, ambitious set of enterprises. Euro Disney s.c.a. has directly or indirectly created 45 000 jobs and has helped to re-establish an equilibrium in the region east of Paris thanks to its rapid growth.

Disneyland® Park: Mad Hatter's Tea Cups.

Disney's NewPort Bay Club®.

Disneyland® Park: Big Thunder Mountain.

Walt Disney Studios® Park.

Walt Disney Studios® Park: Motors' Action! Stunt show.

Disneyland® Park:
Fantasyland décor.

Disneyland® Park:
Sleeping Beauty's castle.

General view of
Disneyland® Resort Paris.

Disneyland® Park:
Main Street, U.S.A.

New cities

THE TWO NEW CITIES in Seine-et-Marne, out of the five created around Paris as of the '60s, now count nearly 330 000 inhabitants. Designed as comprehensive areas to live, they have gradually become focal points for business activity. This is particularly true of Marne-la-Vallée, which is currently the real economic and technological driving force in the region east of Paris. Sénart, the most recent of the new cities, has achieved its dream of becoming a "city in the country" and is just beginning to acquire its economic independence.

Bussy Middle School.

Carré Sénart.

Champs-sur-Marne business activity park.

Plant water tower in Noisiel.

Marne-la-Vallée:
Lognes, "a city in the country".

Land of trade

FAITHFUL TO ITS TRADITION since the Middle Ages, the Seine-et-Marne remains a land of trade and innovation in various fields.
A vast road and railroad network links it to Europe and attracts a large number of high-tech companies.

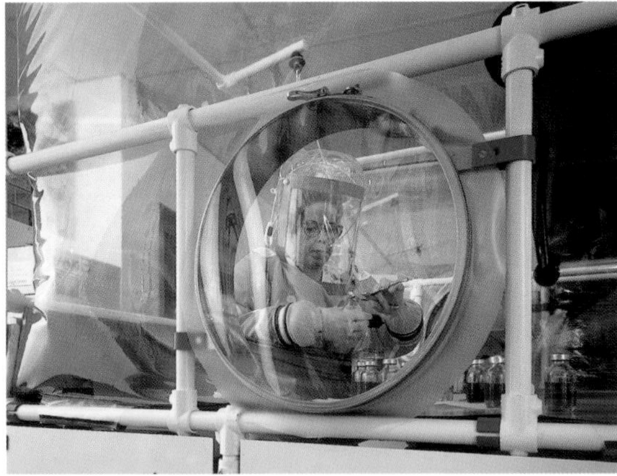

Bristol Meyers Research Laboratory.

Feeder-road 104, la Francilienne.

SAS Institute in Évry-Grécy.

Didier Québecor Printing Works.

Some useful addresses

Seine-et-Marne Departmental Tourist Board

11, rue Royale
77300 Fontainebleau
Tel.: 01 60 39 60 39
Internet: http://www.tourisme77.net

Île-de-France Regional Tourist Board

91, avenue des Champs Elysées
75008 Paris
Tel.: 01 56 89 38 00
Internet: http://www.paris-ile-de-France.com

Espace du Tourisme at Disneyland Resort® Paris

Place François Truffaut
77705 Marne-la-Vallée cedex 04
Tel.: 01 60 43 33 33
Internet: http://www.tourisme77 and www.paris-ile-de-France.com

Departmental Division of Archives and Heritage

248, avenue Charles Prieur
77190 Dammarie-lès-Lys
Tel.: 01 64 87 37 00

Departmental Île-de-France Prehistory Museum

48, avenue de Stalingrad
77140 Nemours
Tel.:01 64 78 54 80

Stéphane Mallarmé Departmental Museum

4, quai S. Mallarmé
77870 Vulaines-sur-Seine
Tel.: 01 64 23 73 27

Departmental Museum of the Lands of Seine-et-Marne

77750 Saint-Cyr-sur-Morin
Tel.: 01 60 24 46 00

This book was published
under the ægis of the
Conseil Général de Seine-et-Marne and the Departmental Tourist Board
and with the assistance of the
Espace du Tourisme d'Île-de-France et de Seine-et-Marne
at Disneyland Resort® Paris

We thank for their collaboration

Jean-Bernard Roy, *Curator of the Île-de-France Prehistory Museum,*
Amaury Lefébure, *Chief Curator of the Museum and National Domain of Fontainebleau Castle,*
Jean-Louis Charpentier, *General Curator of the Heritage in charge of managing the domains of Champs and Jossigny,*
Mireille Munch, *Curator of Ferrières Castle,* Danielle Magnan, *Regional Archeological Service,*
Annie-Claire Lussiez, *Curator of the Municipal Museum of Melun,*
Denis Vassigh, *Facilitator of the Heritage Service, Art and History, of the town of Meaux,*
Léopold Sarteau, *President of the Departmental Federation for fisheries and the protection of aquatic areas,*
the Regional Nature Reserve of the French Gâtinais, Seine-et-Marne Développement, The Friends of Alfred Sisley
and all the owners of private homes who kindly opened their doors to us.

Credit for photography

Gilles Adnot, Jean-François Benard, Patrick Cadet © CMN Paris, Jean-François Caltot, Jean-Pierre Chasseau, Philippe de Murel, Laurent Devillers, © Disney, François Doury, Georges Fessy, Jean Paul Houdry, Michel Huot, Roland Jo, Pascal Lemaître © CMN, Paris, Famille Lerou, Danielle Magnan, Fabrice Milochau, Bernard Pamard, Jean-François Phalipon, Jean-Paul Planchon, Bernard Plessy, Léopold Sarteau, Christian Voisin, Île-de-France Prehistory Museum in Nemours, Municipal Museum of Melun, Conseil Général de Seine-et-Marne, Seine-et-Marne Développement, Seine-et-Marne Tourist Office, Provins Tourist Office, City of Meaux - Heritage Service - Art and History, The Minneapolis Institute of Art, Regional Nature Reserve of the French Gâtinais, IAURIF, Arelys.

Téléphone : 05 61 83 95 78 – Télécopie : 05 61 83 97 90
E-mail : edd.briand@wanadoo.fr

Graphic design and layout Georges Rivière — Studio Stéphan Arcos
Photoengraving TEC
Printing SYL

English version
Translation Sarah Combette-Molson
Coordination Chantal Inard

Printed in the European Community

Text
Jean-François Caltot, *Journalist*

Editorial and Supervisory Committee

Jean-François Robinet	*President of Seine-et-Marne Tourist Board*
Jean-Luc Michaud	*President of the Espace du Tourisme d'Île de France et de Seine-et-Marne*
Laurence Picard	*Conseiller Général, President of the Tourism Commission*
Jean-Pierre Pineau	*Chief of Communication and External Relations of the Conseil Général*
Laurent Devillers	*Director of the Espace du Tourisme d'Île-de-France et de Seine-et-Marne*
Isabelle Rambaud	*Director of the Archives and Heritage*
Christiane Schaefer	*Chief of Press Relations of Seine-et-Marne Tourist Board*
Jean-Pierre Chasseau	*Photographer*

Coordination of the work
Jean-François Robinet and Christiane Schaefer